Exercises for Management Reflection

The Servant-Leader Workbook

Joseph M. Patrnchak

THE ENGAGED ENTERPRISE: THE SERVANT-LEADER WORKBOOK

ISBN 13: 978-1-944338-07-7

Book design by Adam Robinson

Published by The Greenleaf Center for Servant Leadership
133 Peachtree St. NE, Suite 350
Atlanta, GA 30303
www.greenleaf.org

Joe Patrnchak can be reached at joe@gsummit.co.

CONTENTS

Exercises for Management Reflection

INTRODUCTION

As an HR professional, I've had the privilege of serving as Chief Human Resources Officer of Cleveland Clinic and Blue Cross Blue Shield of Massachusetts, and as VP of Human Resources for the $4.5B Global Customer Services Division of HP/Compaq/Digital. In each of those roles, my core mission was to help the organization bring out the very best in our people.

Since 2014, I've continued to pursue that mission as Principal of Green Summit Partners, LLC. While the organizations I work with now are highly diverse, their core challenge is essentially the same: how to create a culture that fosters high levels of employee engagement.

Why is employee engagement such a critical issue? Because high engagement has been proven to drive superior performance in virtually every critical metric, including revenue, profitability, and customer satisfaction.

As a tool to help with this mission, I wrote and in 2016 published *The Engaged Enterprise: A Field Guide for the Servant -Leader*. Basically, the book lays out five core principles that I believe are critical to successful organizational change and the development of a highly engaged workforce. Here's an overview of those principles.

1. Real Change Starts with Real Dissatisfaction.

Let's say that you've concluded that your organization needs to change if it's going to build a highly engaged workforce. You know you can't make that change happen by yourself: you're going to need buy-in from people all across the organization, especially the senior leadership team.

But you also know that some of those people will resist, because change always provokes resistance. So what do you do?

You leverage dissatisfaction with the organization's performance to build a strong business case for change. That may sound easy, but it's not—and it also comes with some very real risk—but if you want real change, it's necessary.

2. When A Mission Becomes Personal, It Becomes A Cause.

While people will certainly work to achieve a mission, they'll give everything they have for a cause. So how do you personalize your organization's mission? How do you turn it into a cause that really inspires and engages your people?

You can use your institutional vocabulary to help connect your employees to your mission. At Cleveland Clinic, for example, we changed how we referred to our employees. Today all Clinic employees are referred to as caregivers, whether they're doctors, nurses, or work in facilities, the kitchen, or accounting. This may not sound like a big deal, but I'm sure it played a big part in driving up engagement.

3. If You Don't Care, They Won't Care.

The most important single driver of employee engagement is whether or not employees feel that their leaders, at every level, really care about them. So how do you create a caring mindset in your organization's leaders?

One idea is to adopt servant leadership principles to balance and, when appropriate, replace the traditional command-and-control model.

Servant leaders see their role as helping others succeed. They listen more, share decision-making, rely on persuasion, and go out of their way to recognize the work of others. To get your organization's leaders to buy into servant leadership, you need to build the business case—starting with the fact that "servant-led" companies outperform their competition on a wide variety of metrics. Don't expect every leader to buy in right away, but if you keep pushing the rock, you'll see amazing results.

4. Old Habits Die Hard, So Hardwire the Change.

Organizational change initiatives all too often start strong then fade away. To avoid falling into this trap you have to keep talking about what needs to change—and hold your leaders at every level accountable for sustaining the change process. At Cleveland Clinic, for example, we required every leader to have an engagement plan for their organization, with clear metrics, and with a significant part of their performance evaluation (and compensation) tied to those metrics.

5. It's About Building Pyramids, Not Sandcastles.

Successful lasting change takes time. If you're committed to building and sustaining an engaged enterprise, you'll need to keep making the business case for change when others turn their attention elsewhere. By the way, that can happen when the initial results aren't all that exciting, but it can also happen when you get a quick boost in your engagement scores. If you want to build long-term success, don't let anyone convince you that "We tried, but this just won't work," or, conversely, "Ok, we made some changes and got good results, so we can move on to the next challenge."

A Tool for Management Reflection.

This workbook consists of brief essays on engagement-related topics—topics that are largely based on the questions leaders ask me when we discuss how to move their organizations toward higher levels of engagement. The essays originally appeared on my blog, although some of them have been slightly modified here. I've also added a few questions at the end of each essay to help stimulate your thinking.

These essay/exercises are intended as a tool for management reflection, which is just a term for thinking deeply about your business and about your role as a leader. This kind of focused reflection is critical to our development as leaders; it helps to foster the attitudes, beliefs, and emotional intelligence that define us as leaders.

With that in mind, imagine if every day or every other day for a month, you read one of the essays in this workbook, answered the questions associated with it, and wrote out one or two ideas that the essay had stimulated. At the end of the month you could prioritize those ideas, pick out those that seem most powerful, and spend the next month fleshing them out, again for just fifteen to thirty minutes a day. At the end of *that* month, you'd be looking at a pretty exciting action plan for how to really bring out the best in your people and your organization.

Here's another idea. What if you gave a copy of the workbook to some of the leaders in your organization, and once a month you met to discuss just one of the essays? I can almost guarantee that over the course of six, or twelve, or eighteen months, your organization would be in a very different place.

However you choose to use this tool, I hope you'll let me know how it goes. And please visit my website at www.gsummit.co, check out the latest blog entry, and—most of all—join the conversation. I look forward to hearing from you!

—Joe Patrnchak

1. EMPLOYEE ENGAGEMENT...A TIRED TOPIC?

Someone recently suggested to me that "Employee engagement has been written about and talked about so much that it's really a tired topic." I've heard this before, and in part I think it's a reflection of our culture's obsession with the Next New Thing. Whether it's the latest political crisis, celebrity scandal, electronic toy—our individual and collective attention span seems to constantly grow shorter.

The real issue here, it seems to me, is that for as much as employee engagement has been researched and written about over the past ten or more years, the fact is that we still haven't come close to solving the engagement problem. According to Gallup, which has been tracking employee engagement in the US since 2000, less than one third of US employees are engaged in their jobs. Nearly 20% are "actively disengaged," which by Gallup's definition means they "aren't just unhappy at work; they're busy acting out their unhappiness. Every day these workers undermine what their engaged co-workers accomplish."

So basically what this means is that two out of three employees in the US go to work without feeling a strong emotional and intellectual connection to their organization, their job, and their colleagues—the kind of connection that leads to their putting in that extra effort to get the job done right. Is there any doubt that this has a negative effect on performance?

It seems that the issue is not that employee engagement is a tired topic. The problem is that most organizations haven't solved their engagement problem. Given how much has been written on the subject, why is that?

I think it's because creating—and sustaining—the kind of culture that produces high engagement is just plain hard. And most leadership teams don't do the hard work to make it happen. They may put raising engagement on their list of goals for the year, but all too often they don't include it in the strategic plan. Or if it is included, it rarely receives top-of-mind status within the plan or at executive or board meetings. This in spite of the compelling research that highly engaged organizations perform better across most of the dimensions within those strategic plans.

The fact is that building an engaged workforce means addressing or changing your culture, which is difficult and takes time. It's not enough to get excited and implement some new benefits or other employee-focused programs. While this may bump up an organization's engagement scores in the short term, all too often that progress then leads to a loss of momentum. Engagement falls off the radar screen. Managers and employees come to see the engagement initiative as just another "fad" in a long line of fads. The managers slip back into old behaviors that lead to dis-engagement.

What can be done to keep this from happening? No one has all the answers; I know I don't. But I do know that in the organizations I've been part of, we were successful in building and sustaining an engaged workforce only when engagement became an integral part of our strategic plan. When we defined—and tracked—a set of clear engagement metrics. When we gave those metrics visibility at the most senior levels, and managers had at least 25%-40% of their annual review weighted on their progress and achievement of their engagement goals. When engagement received the same level of planning effort as any other major business change effort within the company—and when that plan was communicated as such.

Management Reflections

Use this space to jot down answers to the following questions, and to outline any ideas, plans, or practical first steps you might take to move yourself or your organization forward.

1. *Do YOU think employee engagement is a tired topic?*
2. *Has engagement been discussed "too much" in your organization?*
3. *Does your organization still have an engagement problem?*

2. WHAT'S IN *YOUR* STRATEGIC PLAN?

Pretty much by definition, your organization's strategic plan must include a set of clearly defined objectives—objectives that have been prioritized, operationalized, quantified, and cascaded down from the enterprise level to all operating units. Action plans to meet those objectives are drawn up at every level, and performance against those plans is measured and evaluated.

While the process varies from one organization to another, you can't manage an organization of any size and complexity without following the basic steps: define your goals, decide on a plan to meet those goals, measure your progress, and adjust accordingly.

So here's a question: is increased employee engagement a high priority component of your strategic plan? At least, in my experience, in many organizations the answer to that question is "No," despite the fact that research on this subject clearly shows that high engagement correlates positively with a wide array of key metrics, including revenue, profitability, quality, customer satisfaction, and many others.

Frankly, I don't get it.

To me it seems pretty straightforward. Highly engaged employees outperform less engaged employees. Organizations with higher percentages of engaged employees outperform organizations with fewer engaged employees. So if you want to outperform your competition, it follows that you should do whatever you can to build a highly engaged workforce. That's not all you need to do, of course, but it seems obvious that it's definitely one of the key things you need to do.

Which means you need to treat engagement like all the other components of your strategic plan. You need to set engagement targets at every level, develop action plans to hit those targets, measure performance in a systematic way, and hold managers at every level accountable for the results they deliver.

If your organization is already doing all that, great. If it's not already happening—and you're not yet at the level where you can make it happen across the entire organization—don't forget that *You are the CEO of your own organization.*

While many things need to occur at the enterprise in order to build a truly engaged enterprise, it's also true that engagement is built day in and day out, by managers and supervisors and team leaders at the small unit level.

Which means that even if you're leading a small unit within a larger enterprise, you can—and should—create and implement your own engagement strategy. The results could set an example for other leaders, and maybe even set a much wider change in motion.

Management Reflections

Use this space to jot down answers to the following questions, and to outline any ideas, plans, or practical first steps you might take to move yourself or your organization forward.

1. *Does your organization's strategic plan have a "people" component?*
2. *Is employee engagement a regular topic of discussion at your regular leadership meetings?*
3. *Are leaders in your organization evaluated against engagement metrics, just like other key business metrics?*
4. *Is anything preventing your organization's leaders from recognizing employee engagement as a critical strategic issue?*

3. GETTING THE BEST OUT OF YOUR ORGANIZATION: YES, IT DOES TAKE TIME

Recently I met with the executive team of a successful small business that's wrestling with the question of how to achieve even higher levels of employee engagement, organizational performance, and customer satisfaction. As we discussed what it might take to achieve their goals, the head of customer service said,

"These steps we're discussing...like giving our people more support and mentoring... they absolutely make sense, but how are we...the people in this room...going to fit them into our day to day workload, when we're already overstretched?"

It's a question I've heard many times because the fact is leaders at every level, in pretty much every organization, are always pressed for time. They—you—are constantly under pressure to get things done, to complete those projects, make those numbers, hit those performance goals. With too many meetings to attend and too many fires to put out, there never seems to be enough hours in the day. So how do you find the time to get to know the people in your organization and give them the support they need to develop their potential? How do you find the time to build a culture that fosters high levels of engagement?

Obviously, the answer lies in how you set priorities—where you choose to spend more time and where you choose to spend less. Which brings me to the difference between managing and leading. A great deal has been written on this subject, but in my mind, managing is more about organizing people, controlling costs, and deploying resources. Leadership, on the other hand, is more about motivating, inspiring, and bringing out the best in people. It's about helping people expand their vision of what's possible, and then helping them achieve that vision. That takes time—time spent meeting with people, listening to them, and figuring out how to remove the barriers that get in the way of their performing to their full potential.

So if you're wondering where you'll find the time to do the hard work of building a culture of engagement, you might ask yourself, "If I'm really a leader, what else should I be doing?"

As you think about that, here's something else you might want to consider. When the customer service leader quoted above raised the "time" issue, one of the other people in the room said, "That's a good point. But what if we each put 10% of our time into getting more out of the other people in the organization...and as a result they each got 10% more productive... wouldn't the whole company be much better off?"

Good point, don't you think?

The fact is that building an engaged culture does take time. As a leader, you can't afford *not* to find that time.

Management Reflections

Use this space to jot down answers to the following questions, and to outline any ideas, plans, or practical first steps you might take to move yourself or your organization forward.

1. *How much time do you think you now spend on "people issues?"*
2. *What's keeping you from spending more time thinking about how to create a culture that encourages high engagement?*
3. *How can you re-prioritize to free up more time?*

4. EMPLOYEE SATISFACTION. EMPLOYEE MORALE. EMPLOYEE ENGAGEMENT. WHAT'S THE DIFFERENCE? DOES IT MATTER?

Let me start by saying that while these terms do overlap, there are differences among them. Do those differences really matter? They do, if you're trying to build an organization that delivers extraordinary results.

OK, so let's take a closer look at these concepts, starting with job satisfaction, which seems to me the most basic of the three because it refers simply to how content employees are with their work environment, benefits etc. It answers the question "Are you comfortable?" The problem is that a high level of job satisfaction doesn't necessarily mean that an organization is getting truly outstanding performance from its employees.

It's definitely possible for an employee to be satisfied with his/her job but not be a particularly high performer. People can get comfortable in their performance zone. They feel safe there, and not particularly challenged. For some people, though—and in my experience, this includes your "high potentials" and many "millennials"—this safe, secure feeling isn't enough. If these people don't feel challenged, they will eventually get bored and leave. They'll move to an organization where their leaders *expect* them to be better than average and work hard to help them get there. For these people—the people most likely to take your organization to new heights—job satisfaction is nice, but it's not enough.

Employee morale goes a step beyond job satisfaction, implying a greater sense of purpose and a more direct connection to performance. It's hard to imagine someone saying of their organization, "Our employees have really high morale, but they don't perform well," or vice versa. Morale, however, can change quickly when difficult times set in, if the foundations to sustain it are not in place. I hate to compare efforts to raise morale to "pep rallies," but that's all too often what they resemble.

If you're really trying to build a high performance organization, I think you need to go beyond thinking about employee morale. You need to be thinking about employee engagement. Why? Because employee engagement includes not only how comfortable your employees are and how they're feeling in the short term, but also whether or not they feel a strong emotional and intellectual connection with their work and their organization. And here's the really important thing: with highly engaged employees, that connection motivates them to put extra effort into what they do on the job.

That discretionary effort is what employee engagement is all about. It's what takes you from ok performance, or even good performance, to great performance. It's what sees you through the difficult times—and difficult times always come.

So let's sum up. Job satisfaction and high morale are important, but they're not enough—not in today's hyper competitive business environment. These days we can't afford to set the bar that low. We need to build that strong intellectual and emotional connection between our employees and our organization.

We need them to feel that the organization's mission is their own personal cause, to the point where they do the ordinary things exceptionally well, and sometimes even do things that go beyond the ordinary.

That's the goal we should all be setting for the organizations we lead, because organizations that have high levels of engagement consistently outperform their competition. (The research is rich with evidence on this.) But the other reason is that it's just so much more fun to come to work every day when you and the people around you feel connected to something bigger than yourselves, when you're all pushing yourselves and one another to be better.

So don't settle for just job satisfaction or good morale. Don't sleep walk through your career as a leader and let your employees settle for OK performance. The people you serve are better than that and so are you.

Management Reflections

Use this space to jot down answers to the following questions, and to outline any ideas, plans, or practical first steps you might take to move yourself or your organization forward.

1. *Do your people give that "discretionary extra effort" on a regular basis?*
2. *If more of your employees gave that extra effort on a regular basis, what would that look like?*
3. *What effect would that extra effort have on the business?*

5. I HAVE A COUPLE OF PEOPLE IN MY ORGANIZATION THAT I JUST CAN'T SEEM TO ENGAGE. WHAT SHOULD I DO?

I hear this question all the time, from managers at many organizational levels. It can be very frustrating when no matter how hard you try, there are still some people who just cannot or will not get on the bus. What's even worse is when they even seem to be working against you. According to Gallup's research, it actually takes four actively engaged employees to neutralize just one actively disengaged person. From your own experience I think you'd agree that these people can really suck the energy out of an organization, when you consider all the workarounds you have to come up with to offset their negativity, all the complaints about their attitude you have to deal with from their teammates. And sometimes what makes the situation even more complicated is that these people may even be achieving the business goals set in front of them.

So what do you do?

My first recommendation is to understand that as a leader you can't actually engage any employee. After all my years as an HR leader working to build engaged organizations, I've come to the conclusion that as a leader all you can do is work hard to create the kind of environment in which employees want to get engaged.

What I'm saying is that getting engaged at work… or not getting engaged at work…is a choice, a decision, that only the employee can make.

The fact is that there will always be some employees who choose not to be engaged no matter what you do, and at some point it's not worth banging your head against the wall trying to figure out why. You're a leader, not a psychologist, and you probably won't figure it out anyway, because more often than not these folks don't understand why themselves.

So again, what do you do? I always recommend making attitude just as important a performance issue as any other business goal. This means actively managing the employee by having frequent performance discussions that include their lack of engagement and negative attitude.

During those discussions—which you should document—you provide direct feedback about what you mean by a negative attitude, how that attitude affects the organization, and where it could lead if their attitude doesn't improve. And where it could lead is that you might have to ask that person to get off the bus.

By the way, frequent performance discussions that include engagement issues should be part of your management process with everyone in your organization, so that the disengaged employee will not be surprised or feel singled out when you have this discussion. I've had many emotional meetings with managers who have had it with an employee! Something tipped the scale, it was the last straw, and they want to fire the person. But when I ask for documentation around their performance discussions with that person, all too often it's shallow or even non-existent.

Contrary to what managers think, you *can* move an employee out of your organization for a negative attitude, just as for any other performance issue. But you have to do it in a way that is fair and compliant.

I realize that none of this is easy: dismissing an employee never is. But being a leader is not an easy job. And remember, no matter how hard you work at building an environment where employees want to be engaged, you'll be judged not only by what you do, but what kind of behavior you tolerate in the organization. Which means that when you finally do ask those disengaged people to get off the bus, you should be prepared for the silent cheer that will go up from the rest of your organization!

Management Reflections

Use this space to jot down answers to the following questions, and to outline any ideas, plans, or practical first steps you might take to move yourself or your organization forward.

1. *Does your organization include attitude in your performance management system?*
2. *If not, are you actively managing attitude?*
3. *What positive effect would it have on your organization if some people were asked to "get off the bus?"*

6. WATCH YOUR LANGUAGE!

If you're trying to understand—or change—an organization's culture, one important leverage point is the **institutional language.** This is the array of words and phrases that appear consistently, although often unconsciously, when people in the organization make reference to its employees, leaders, customers, practices, etc. Institutional language is important because it is grounded in a set of values and beliefs which is then communicated throughout the organization when you use that language.

When the challenge is to build a truly engaged enterprise, the language related to employees is particularly important. For example, I've worked in organizations that referred to their employees as either "professional staff" or "non-professional" staff. Whatever other purpose this distinction may have served, I'm pretty sure that it didn't encourage the so-called "non-professionals" to bring their A-game to work every day.

And just think about those newscasts we've all seen in which government officials, faced with a major weather event, announce that all "non-essential personnel" have been told to stay home from work. Think about it: how would you feel about going to work every day for an organization that regards you as "non-essential?"

A public relations executive colleague of mine once told me, "Never use internal language you wouldn't want your customers to discover, especially when you might be referring to them." It's interesting that we generally take great care to examine our "customer-facing" language, but rarely think much about how we talk about and to the people who serve those customers.

Of course, you might be thinking that this is much ado about nothing. You might be asking, does the institutional language we use really matter all that much? While working on a journal article, I found an interesting article[1] by the CEO of the Arizona Girl Scouts organization that dealt with this question. After a survey revealed that many of the organization's volunteers felt that the organization did not trust them, the CEO took a hard look at its institutional vocabulary. For example, in a four-page brochure used to recruit volunteers, she found the words "must," "mandatory," or "required" used a combined 84 times. Ultimately she concluded: *"In our zeal to promote the health and safety of girls, we had unknowingly used command-and-control language that implicitly communicated that we did not trust our volunteers to make their own decisions in the best interests of the girls."*

Speaking more broadly, she then added: *"…we discovered just how powerfully our own language had influenced and contributed to our organizational culture. We are still debating whether the language described or created the culture. Perhaps it did both."*

So yes, institutional language does matter.

When Cleveland Clinic made the commitment to build a culture that fostered high levels of employee engagement, we made a number of changes to our own institutional vocabulary—the most important of which was to substitute "caregiver" for "employee" in all of our communications. Our ID badges were changed to

1 *Building organizational culture—word by word*; T J. Woodbury. Available at: http://onlinelibrary.wiley.com/doi/10.1002/ltl.165/abstract.

say "caregiver," and "We are all caregivers" became our mantra, even appearing as the title of our annual report. The message was transmitted repeatedly on our internal communications media, and reinforced by managers at every level in their meetings and presentations.

The rationale for the change was simply that everyone who worked at the Clinic had the potential to create a positive—or negative—experience for a patient, family member, or colleague. Not only the doctors and nurses, but also the people who delivered the patient's meals or cleaned their rooms or answered questions about a bill—everyone had a role in creating a positive, or negative, experience for our patients and their families. The transporter who helped reassure a nervous patient on the way for a test procedure, the facilities worker who asked a family member who looked a little lost if they needed help, the admissions person who answered questions with patience—all of these people were "giving care."

And this isn't just something that applies to hospitals and other non-profit organizations. Whether the organization provides a product or a service, everyone in the organization is important to living out its mission. Everyone has to see themselves in the value chain of serving a customer directly or serving someone who is an internal customer. When people see themselves this way, you have the starting point for a truly engaged enterprise. When they don't....

But here's the thing: it's important, but not sufficient, to use the right language. As a leader, you have to go out every day and earn the right to use that language. You've got to "walk the talk." If you want to make it clear that everyone in your organization matters and has a role to play in the organization's success, it's not enough to start referring to employees as "associates" while continuing to treat them as replaceable cogs in a wheel.

At Cleveland Clinic we took whatever steps we could to reinforce the idea of "We are all caregivers." We established a highly popular caregiver wellness program and a recognition program that celebrated the little things that our caregivers did every day. We created the Caregiver Experience Program, in which we took all 43,000 caregivers off line over a nine-month period to meet in small, cross-functional groups—groups that included staff from every level and function, including physicians and senior executives—to talk explicitly how each of their roles touched our patients. And when we were forced to close one of our community hospitals, we worked very hard to place 90% of the caregivers from that facility into other jobs within our system.

The result? Our engagement surveys, and perhaps more importantly, our patient feedback, made it clear that our new institutional language did indeed resonate with our people, and did make a difference in how they felt about their work and how they actually performed that work.

So once again, language does matter. As a professor of psychology at Stanford commented in an article[2] on the relationship between language and thinking: "... it turns out that if you change how people talk, that changes how they think." And changing how people think is the first step to changing how they act.

Which brings me to you and your organization? Does your institutional language need to change? Does it encourage or discourage engagement? Is it as empowering as it could be? Are your employee handbook and policies loaded with command and control language—"must," "required," "cause for dismissal," etc.? What about the language you personally use every day at work?

2 *Lost in Translation*; L. Boroditsky; Wall Street Journal. Available at: http://lera.ucsd.edu/papers/wsj.pdf.

Management Reflections

Use this space to jot down answers to the following questions, and to outline any ideas, plans, or practical first steps you might take to move yourself or your organization forward.

1. *Is there any institutional language in your organization that might not be bringing out the best in people?*
2. *Is there any institutional language that you wouldn't want your customers to hear?*
3. *How could you replace or otherwise change that language?*

7. A BETTER WAY TO LEAD

Most employees are not going to really care about their work or their organization's customers until they themselves feel cared for. In other words, **if you don't care, they won't care**.

But what makes an employee feel that their organization does in fact care about them? The research on employee engagement is actually a great place to start looking for an answer to this question. One study of engagement, conducted by the Dale Carnegie organization, notes:

"...engaged employees lead to happy, loyal customers and repeat business...although there are multiple factors affecting engagement, the personal relationship between a manager and his or her direct reports is the most influential."

Of course, this relationship between supervisor and employee has many dimensions, and it's worth noting that many of the factors that go into the relationship have themselves been identified as key drivers of engagement. These include:

- Stimulating work
- Opportunities for professional development
- Having his/her opinions listened to
- Recognition for good work.

Clearly, a direct supervisor plays a critical—a "direct"—role in each of these areas.

So here's the question: how can an organization get its direct supervisors—and in fact, its leaders at every level—to put time and effort into making sure that their employees have the opportunity to develop new skills and do stimulating work, have their opinions listened to, and receive the recognition they deserve? And what might happen if you and your organization embraced a leadership model that demonstrated this kind of caring for your people every day.

All of which brings me to Servant-Leadership.

Servant-leaders put their people and their organization first, well ahead of their own prerogatives as the "boss." Servant-leaders share power and decision-making as much as possible. Instead of harping on the weaknesses of the people who work for them, they build on their strengths, providing opportunities for professional development and stretch assignments. Servant-leaders listen to the opinions and ideas of others, regardless of position. They co-create solutions, tapping into the collective genius of the people in their organizational unit. And servant-leaders direct the spotlight away from themselves and onto others, sharing recognition or giving it away entirely. Finally, they do this with high levels of emotional intelligence!

The result? Servant-led organizations (which include industry leaders like Zappos, Southwest Airlines, Marriott, and Starbucks) outperform their competitors across a whole range of key performance metrics.

The bottom line? For me, at least, it's simply this: *Servant-leadership is a better way to lead!*

Management Reflections

Use this space to jot down answers to the following questions, and to outline any ideas, plans, or practical first steps you might take to move yourself or your organization forward.

1. *Do leaders across your organization generally act as if they care about their people?*
2. *What specific decisions or actions have your organization's leaders taken that might make employees feel that they are valued? Or not valued?*
3. *What comes to mind when you hear the term "servant leader?"*
4. *What might stand in the way of your organization's implementing servant leadership?*

8. THE SERVANT-LEADER JOURNEY

Servant-Leadership has been at the core of my work for many years. One reason is simply that at a gut level the idea of the leader as servant just seems "right" to me, but equally important is the fact that servant-leadership "works," as indicated by research that consistently shows that "servant-led" enterprises significantly outperform other organizations.

I first became exposed to the idea of the leader as servant nearly twenty years ago when I became VP of HR for Digital Equipment's $3.5B Global Service Business. After five years of downsizing and restructuring, we needed to build a new people strategy to re-engage a workforce that operated in 114 countries, and I was asked to lead this critical initiative. One of my colleagues, who had been Director of Quality at Xerox, introduced me to the work being done on the "service profit chain" by a group of professors at Harvard Business School. Their groundbreaking book[3] on the subject made a powerful impression on me—so powerful in fact that the ideas it laid out ultimately became central to our new people strategy.

The book articulated the economic power of developing not just satisfied customers, but *loyal* customers. Loyal customers feel an emotional connection to your service or product and your brand—an emotional connection created by highly engaged employees. Because of that emotional connection, loyal customers are six times more likely to be repeat customers. They're also more likely to refer their friends to your business, and they're even willing to pay more for your products or services.

As examples, the authors called out in particular two companies and their leaders: Herb Kelleher from Southwest Airlines and William Pollard from the Service Master Company. Both men consider themselves servant-leaders. Herb talked about loving his people. It wasn't enough to just care about your people, he said. You have to *love* your people. (The company's NYSE symbol is LUV.)

To Bill Pollard, leading with a servant's heart meant being willing to do any job in the company as confirmation that all work, even the most mundane, is important. (At least four times a year, all the executives at Service Master go out to clean offices side by side with their work crews.) To Bill, leading with a servant's heart also meant being willing to step back and give others credit and visibility when it's the best thing for their development.

I found the interviews with these two iconic CEOs fascinating and compelling, and they inspired me to learn more about this notion of a "Leader as a Servant." That led me to the work of Robert Greenleaf.

Greenleaf spent nearly forty years at ATT, serving among other assignments as the company's designated "troubleshooter" and Director of Management Development. In 1970 he published *The Servant as Leader*, and until his death in 1990 he dedicated himself to spreading the gospel of servant leadership. Through Greenleaf's writings and the work of others, I took myself to school on the topic. Eventually, I had the opportunity to put servant-leadership at the

3 *The Service Profit Chain: How Leading Companies Link Profit and Growth to Loyalty, Satisfaction, and Value*; J. Heskett, W. Sasser, L. Schlesinger.

core of the people strategy at Cleveland Clinic, with dramatic results.

When I became CHRO at Cleveland Clinic in December of 2007, the Clinic was (as it continues to be) renowned for its outstanding clinical results and medical breakthroughs. Nonetheless, the Clinic's performance back then in terms of patient satisfaction did not match its reputation. When the results of the Federal government's first patient experience survey (the so-called "HCHAPS") came out in 2008, the Clinic's overall rating was just average, and its scores on the individual metrics were below average across the board. In the CEO's words, "People come to us, we save their lives, but they don't like us very much."

Not surprisingly, at least to anyone who understood the service profit chain, the Clinic also had a serious employee engagement problem. When we commissioned Gallup to do an engagement survey in 2008, our scores were only in the 44th percentile of large healthcare systems.

To turn the situation around we launched a series of enterprise initiatives, some focused directly on the patient experience but many focused on improving employee engagement. We changed our institutional language to refer to everyone at the Clinic as a "caregiver." This reminded us in a small but important way that we were all in the value chain of delivering care and creating a safe, supportive experience for our patients and their families. Not just our physicians and nurses, but our food service workers, facilities staff, and people who transported patients around the hospital.

We also launched a new caregiver wellness program, a new caregiver recognition program, and significant upgrades to an array of benefit programs. Equally important was the gradual implementation of servant leader training for leaders at every level, from supervisors to top executives.

As these initiatives took hold and became embedded in the culture, caregiver engagement rose to the 87th percentile, and patient satisfaction rose in direct parallel.

I believe servant-leadership brings out the best in leaders and creates organizations that bring out the best in their people. That's why I believe it's an idea whose time has come, and why I hope you'll take the time to learn more about how to develop your own servant-leadership skills and those of the other leaders in your organization.

Management Reflections

Use this space to jot down answers to the following questions, and to outline any ideas, plans, or practical first steps you might take to move yourself or your organization forward.

1. *Where are you now on your personal journey to becoming a servant leader?*
2. *Describe the best leader you ever worked for?*
3. *What did it feel like to work for that leader?*

9. SERVANT-LEADERSHIP...WHY DO *YOU* LEAD?

During my career, I've spent a fair amount of time talking to other people about *their* careers, and these conversations almost always come around to the question of leadership. Whether I'm talking to a young person looking to move into their first leadership role, or a VP looking to advance to SVP, I'm always curious about why that person wants to become a leader or wants to take on more leadership responsibility. I'm curious because I've found that how people answer these questions provides a good clue to what kind of leader they are, or will become.

Interestingly, many people have difficulty explaining why they want to lead. Virtually no one says, "I want to make more money" or "I want to have more power," although I'd be surprised if those factors weren't involved in at least some cases. The answers that do finally emerge seem to fall into several broad categories.

The first is the idea that leadership is a *right*. The people whose motivations fall into this category are basically saying "I deserve to move into this leadership role because..." What comes next varies, of course. They deserve more leadership responsibility because they've made their numbers, completed their MBA, been in their present position long enough (or too long), etc. Often this attitude seems to have an undertone of "I've always been a leader...in school, on the playground, on my basketball team, etc." Again, the idea, even if it's never expressed in so many words, seems to be, "I have a right to lead."

A second category, which somewhat overlaps the first, is the idea that leadership is a *rite*, as in rite of passage. The idea here is that the person has passed the various tests and met the various requirements to advance to greater leadership responsibility. The tests and requirements may sound a lot like those mentioned above: i.e. the person has held a certain role for a certain period of time, or completed a certain academic degree or leadership development program, or met some particular performance goal.

A third category is what I call leadership as a *privilege*. People whose motivation seems to fall into this category say things like, "I feel I can provide greater value to the organization if I was offered a broader role." Or, "I'd like to share and leverage what I've learned on XYZ project or in XYZ assignment."

I must say that the idea of leadership as a privilege resonates more with me than the idea of leadership as a right/rite. In my experience, the leaders who've had the most positive effect on their organizations have thought of leadership in this way. Not that these people are completely selfless, but on the whole they put the organization ahead of themselves. They don't take themselves too seriously, and they're careful not to take advantage of their position power at the expense of the people around them. As a friend of mine once said, "They don't take up all the air in the room."

Some of the leaders I've been privileged to work with take the idea of leadership as privilege to another level. They are the servant-leaders, or those who aspire to become servant-leaders. They want to lead so that they can be of greater service to others.

In his 1970 essay entitled *The Servant as Leader*, Robert Greenleaf defined the servant leader's role as "making sure that other people's highest priority needs are being served," noting that "The servant-leader is servant first...That person is sharply different from one who is leader first, perhaps because of the need to assuage an unusual power drive or to acquire material possessions."

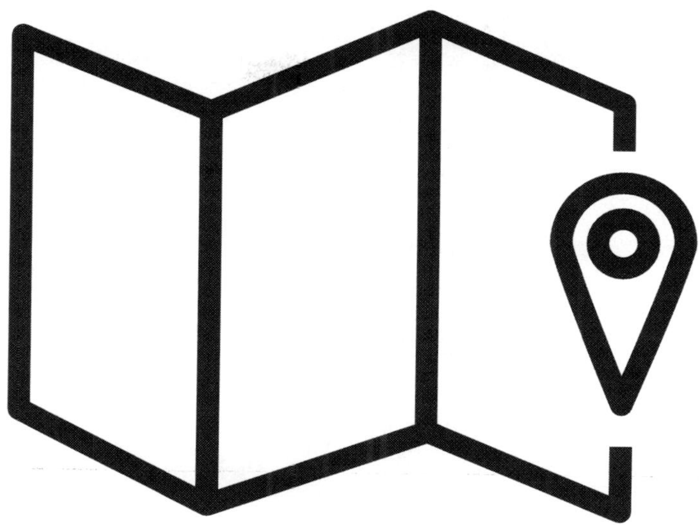

Why do I want to lead? That's the question we all need to think about very deeply. The answer we come to will be critical to the kind of leader we become. The traditional command and control leadership model is grounded in the idea of leadership as a right or a rite. In far too many cases, leaders who operate on the basis of this model and this attitude fall into what I consider the serious error of focusing less on bringing out the best in the organization and its people and more on their own power and prestige.

In premier companies like Southwest Airlines, Starbucks, Zappos, Toro, Nordstrom, Kaiser Permanente, and many others, the leadership model has changed. In these companies, servant-leadership has emerged as an alternative to the traditional command and control model. In these organizations, the leaders see their roles as a privilege—given to them by the people they lead, and in a very real sense, shared with those people. These leaders believe—and act as if—they have to earn the privilege of being a leader every day.

All of which raises the question: "Why do *you* want to lead?" The implications of that question, and how you answer it, are huge, for you and your career, and equally important, for the success of your organization and its people.

Management Reflections

Use this space to jot down answers to the following questions, and to outline any ideas, plans, or practical first steps you might take to move yourself or your organization forward.

1. *Why did you or do you want to become a leader?*
2. *What is your personal definition of leadership?*
3. *What personal values are most critical to you as a leader? What effect do those values have on the people you lead and the organization as a whole?*

10. LEADING AS A SERVANT... EXPLORING YOUR FEAR

Whenever I have the opportunity to talk to a group about Servant-Leadership, someone almost always comes up to me afterward and says something like this:

"The idea of servant-leadership is very appealing. But I work for a boss, and for an organization that's very much about command and control. I'm afraid that if I start to practice servant-leadership, I'll be seen as a weak leader. I could get sidetracked when it comes to promotion. I could even lose my job. I'm not sure what to do."

That's a tough situation to be in. Are you facing a similar challenge?

Let me say first that there's absolutely nothing weak or soft about servant-leadership. Does anybody really think that Herb Kelleher—a dedicated servant-leader—built Southwest Airlines into an industry leader by being weak? Did the servant-leaders who've built organizations like Starbucks and Toro and Marriott and Zappos do it by being soft or weak? I don't think so.

Yes, servant-leadership is about caring for the people in your organization. Caring about their opinions, their wellbeing, and their growth. That means not only giving them opportunities to grow, it means helping them grow by raising the bar, having high expectations for their performance, and holding them accountable for meeting those expectations.

Nothing soft about any of that.

There's no question, however, that if you work in a command and control environment, and you start behaving like a servant-leader—being more collaborative, giving your people more room to take initiative, even more room to make mistakes—there will be an initial transition period. The people you lead will wonder, "What's going on? Is she serious about this? How should I react?" They may be slow to trust that you really want them to take more responsibility. They may test your commitment in ways that are not always easy to handle. But trust me, if you stick with the program, eventually your people will get on board and the results will be dramatic.

But what about the other leaders in your organization—including your boss? They may not even notice that you're doing anything different. In other words, your fears in this regard may be based on assumptions that just aren't valid. These "manufactured fears" can seem very real, even if they never actually materialize. (I know, because I've had my own share of manufactured fears.)

It's also possible that your boss will notice the change in your leadership style and will initially see it as a sign of weakness. In other words, your fears in this regard may in fact be quite valid. But what will happen when your servant-leadership makes your group more productive? What happens when your group really turns it up a notch, when great people want to come work for you? Will your boss still think you're a weak leader?

Unfortunately, there's no one answer to this question. If your boss cares first and foremost about results, he or she will not only support your servant-leadership but may even start following your example. That's how organizational change builds from within.

On the other hand, your boss may never get it. He or she may focus less on the positive results you're producing as a servant-leader and more on the fact that you're not following his or her example of command and control. If that happens, your fears could be realized: you could get passed over for promotion, lose out on desirable projects or development opportunities, or even lose your job.

But here's the thing: if your organization is so committed to command and control leadership that it can't tolerate a servant-leader who delivers great results, do you really want to work there?

If there's one thing I've learned, it's never to tell people how they should feel! But for what it's worth, I think it's important for each of us to develop our own "true north," our own individual sense of what we stand for and how we should behave. As leaders, that means developing our own "leadership identity." If the organization in which we work won't accept that identity, it may be time for us to move on.

So—is there a risk in becoming a servant-leader if you work in a command and control organization? Sure, there's always a risk in behaving differently. But being a leader always involves risk.

What it comes down to is what kind of leader do you want to be? What kind of leader do you *need* to be in order to follow your true north?

Management Reflections

Use this space to jot down answers to the following questions, and to outline any ideas, plans, or practical first steps you might take to move yourself or your organization forward.

1. *Have you tried leading "as a servant" in the past? What was that like?*
2. *What barriers or resistance, if any, did you encounter when you tried this approach to leadership?*
3. *Which of these barriers were real, as opposed to manufactured out of fear?*

11. FEEDBACK: "THE BREAKFAST OF CHAMPIONS"

If you want to get better at anything, one of the most valuable resources you can have is tough, honest feedback, and one of the most valuable skills you can acquire is the ability to handle that feedback effectively. And when I say "acquire," I mean exactly that, because for most of us, the ability to handle tough feedback is definitely not easy. I'll be the first to admit that this is something I've had to work at for most of my career, and even with all that work, I still sometimes find myself getting defensive when someone is critical of something I've done, or haven't done. Let's face it: we'd all rather hear that we're doing a great job.

But again, if we want to get better at anything—and that includes becoming a better leader—honest feedback is incredibly valuable. So how do you get better at dealing with and profiting from feedback?

The single best piece of advice I've been given in this regard is to change the story you tell yourself when you receive the feedback. Much of our behavior—maybe most of our behavior—is shaped by the stories we tell ourselves. Stories in which we're the hero or the victim, stories in which we're being challenged, or taken advantage of, stories in which we fail or triumph. Often we're not even aware that these stories are playing in the background of our mind, but that only makes them more powerful.

So the next time you get some tough feedback, don't let your mind run the story that you're a victim, that you're facing a threat—a threat to your position, your power, your next performance review, your next raise or next promotion, your relationship with your manager or the people you manage.

Rather, you need tell to yourself that this feedback is a valuable gift that will help you become the best leader you can be. And in my opinion, that means becoming a Servant-Leader, leading with a servant's heart. If you view your role as a servant to your people and your organization, you'll find it much easier to accept and even invite tough feedback in order to keep growing and to provide better service to the people around you. You may not always be comfortable hearing it, but you'll definitely find it easier to listen. And you'll get far more out of what you take in.

After all these years I've found the easiest way to figure out whether someone is a servant leader or not is to observe how well they take feedback. Leaders who can't handle feedback, who are threatened by it, who don't want to hear about how they could improve, who maybe even punish those who dare to suggest that they might not be perfect—those people can't be servant-leaders because their view of the world is that it's all about them! The servant-leader turns that view upside down, says it's all about those whom I serve, and embraces anything that will help him or her serve more effectively.

So there you have it. I'm not saying that learning to accept and work with tough feedback will be easy by any means, but I am saying that you can make it *easier*. If you change your story, you can change how you view feedback. You can get past the defensiveness we all experience because we're human. You can use feedback as a source of energy to dramatically move you and your organization to the next level!

Management Reflections

Use this space to jot down answers to the following questions, and to outline any ideas, plans, or practical first steps you might take to move yourself or your organization forward.

1. *How often do you ask your people, colleagues, or managers for feedback on your leadership?*
2. *How do you respond to feedback when you get it?*
3. *What story do you tell yourself when you receive feedback that isn't positive? How could you change this story to become less defensive?*

12. HOW WILL YOUR PEOPLE VOTE?

Winston Churchill once remarked that, "The best argument against democracy is a five-minute conversation with the average voter." On the other hand, Churchill also said, "It has been said that democracy is the worst form of government except all the others that have been tried."

What it comes down to for me is that the process of voting is a powerful way not only to reach important decisions, but it's also a great learning tool for those in a leadership position. Self-awareness is critical to growing and developing as a leader.

With that in mind, I have a question for you: if you asked the people in your organization to vote on whether or not you're a successful leader, what would they say? And what might you learn from what they say?

Now, to make such an exercise useful, I think you'd want to make the question more specific. I believe strongly that servant-leadership is a better way to lead. I believe that because of the considerable body of research that shows that organizations that apply the principles of servant-leadership consistently outperform their competitors across all key metrics

Most companies, however, are not servant led. Most companies, and most organizations within companies, still adhere to the traditional command and control model. How does servant-leadership differ from command and control? The simple chart below can help answer that question.

Command and Control	**Servant-Leadership**
. Position authority	. Moral authority
. Might makes right	. Puts others first
. Survival of the fittest	. Puts the organization first
. My way is better	. Empowers others
. People are tools	. Welcomes feedback
. The end can justify the means	. Builds consensus
. Who screwed up?	. Seeks solutions not blame

So the high-level question you might want to pose to the people in your organization is: As a leader, where do I fall on a continuum between "pure" command and control and "pure" servant-leadership? But what if you dug down a little deeper? What if you asked these seven simple questions that together can help place you on that leadership continuum? The results of that exercise might be very interesting, don't you think?

Please answer the following questions by using the seven-point scale.

1. [Your Name] often asks for feedback on his/her leadership style, he/she often asks how he/she could better support the people in the organization, and he/she really uses the information?

Command & Control — Servant Leadership

1________2__________3_____________4_________5__________6___________7

2. [Your Name] often takes the mission statement off the wall, talks about it at staff meetings, and discusses what that means for everyone on the team, especially when we face a difficult decision.

Command & Control — Servant Leadership

1________2__________3_____________4_________5__________6___________7

3. [Your Name] does *not* do most of the talking during staff meetings and makes it a point to draw people out to participate, asking for their opinions so as to reach solutions together whenever possible.

Command & Control — Servant Leadership

1________2__________3_____________4_________5__________6___________7

4. [Your Name] seems to consider his/her role as a leader to be a privilege, one that the people in the organization give him/her every day.

Command & Control — Servant Leadership

1________2__________3_____________4_________5__________6___________7

5. When mistakes are made, [Your Name] treats them as learning opportunities for the team and himself/herself instead of looking for someone to blame.

Command & Control — Servant Leadership

1________2__________3_____________4_________5__________6___________7

6. [Your Name] puts people in positions to succeed by giving them roles which play to their strengths.

Command & Control — Servant Leadership

1________2__________3_____________4_________5__________6___________7

7. [Your Name] often allows other members of the team to get recognition which he/she could have received, because it would've been the best thing for their development at that time.

Total Score______ Average Score________

Command & Control 1..................2..............3.................4.................5.............6..............7 **Servant-Leadership**

Management Reflections

Use this space to jot down answers to the following questions, and to outline any ideas, plans, or practical first steps you might take to move yourself or your organization forward.

1. *How does the average score I gave myself compare to the score my team gave me?*
2. *On which specific questions was the difference the greatest between the way I rated myself and the way the others on my team rated me?*
3. *What does this suggest in terms of what I do every day as a leader?*
4. *What specific actions could I take to move myself along the continuum toward servant leadership?*

13. IS ANYONE LISTENING?

The US Presidential election of 2016 was undoubtedly one of the most controversial in some time, regardless of which party or candidate you supported. I suppose it's because so many people feel that our country is at a very important crossroad.

As the election process unfolded, it became very clear that many of us profoundly distrust not only that process but our political culture as a whole. There's a strong sense, cutting across party lines, that "politicians" will say and promise virtually anything to get elected, but that they all too frequently fail to deliver on their promises. There's a sense that politicians, especially those "on the other side,"simply can't be trusted to tell us the truth. Without putting too fine a point on it, they lie.

And underlying all of this, there's a sense that the people who run for office, and get elected to office, just don't listen to us. It's easy to see where that comes from. Just watch any political debate or interview. How often do the candidates answer a question directly, as opposed to shifting over to one of their "talking points"?

Some people say, "Well, that's just the political game. They have to play it that way or their agenda will never be heard." Or, "These questions are complicated, but people don't have patience for complicated answers." Maybe. But let me ask you this: how do you feel when a political figure—or anyone else for that matter—refuses to give a straight answer to an important question?

For myself, when I ask someone a question and they dodge it, I feel that I haven't been listened to and that the person on the other side of the conversation simply can't be trusted. If you want me to trust you, the first thing you need to do is show me the courtesy of really listening to what I have to say. Listening is the foundation on which we can build a trusting relationship.

This is true for all relationships, not just that between political leaders and their constituents. It's certainly true for business leaders. I believe the Servant-Leader model is a better way to lead, but how can you serve your people if you're not really listening to them?

What do I mean by *really* listening? I mean something like what Stephen Covey refers to as "empathic listening." In Covey's words, "In empathic listening, you listen with your ears, but you also, and more importantly, listen with your eyes and with your heart. You listen for feeling, for meaning. You listen for behavior. You use your right brain as well as your left. You sense, you intuit, you feel."

As Covey points out, "Most people do not listen with the intent to understand; they listen with the intent to reply. They're either speaking or preparing to speak." That's a habit we have to work hard to overcome.

How do you do that? Start by being present with your people, making eye contact and doing your best to remain non-judgmental during the discussion. Avoid distractions: don't look at your watch or check your e-mail, and turn your phone off. (I know, that sounds ridiculously obvious, but people do this stuff all the time.) Try as hard as you can not to think of your response while the other person is talking. Speak less.

Try to remember the words of the Greek philosopher Epictetus, who said, "We have two ears and one mouth, so we can listen twice as much as we speak."

And when you do speak, be honest. Yes, it's true that as a leader at any level of an organization, you need to be sensitive to the "politics" of the organization, and sometimes that means being careful about what you say and to whom you say it. But it's also true that if you're trying to build trust and high engagement across your organization, you have to start by really listening to people, and you have to be honest when you respond. People may not always like what they hear, but they'll know your position and they'll have a better idea of how to predict your reactions in the future—both critical to building trust.

So, once again, it comes down to this: you can't be an effective leader if your people don't trust you, and your people won't trust you if you don't listen to them. You don't always have to agree with them, or do what they want you to do, but you have to respect them by listening to them and really hearing them.

Management Reflections

Use this space to jot down answers to the following questions, and to outline any ideas, plans, or practical first steps you might take to move yourself or your organization forward.

1. *How do you demonstrate to your people that you're really listening to them?*
2. *What distractions tend to take your attention from those to whom you're speaking?*
3. *Do you sometimes, or even often, check your e-mail and voice mail during meetings?*

14. IT'S NOT JUST ABOUT BUILDING TRUST...IT'S ABOUT BUILDING BELIEF!

Trust matters. No organization—whether it's a small business, a Fortune 100 global giant, or the government of a nation—can function effectively over the long term unless its people basically believe that its leaders can generally be trusted to speak the truth and do the right thing. That's undoubtedly why I'm so often asked by leaders I meet with, "How can I build greater trust in my organization among our employees?"

I think the answer is embedded in the last paragraph. If you want to build trust among your employees, you have to change what they believe about your organization. More specifically, you need to create an environment that encourages your employees to hold these five critical beliefs:

- "I believe our leaders are genuinely connected to the mission of the organization, and put that mission first in their decision making."
- "I believe our leaders are thoughtful in their decision making."
- "I believe our leaders care about me and what's important to me."
- "I believe our leaders value and respect my opinion."
- "I believe our leaders understand and appreciate what it takes to get my job done."

How do you build these beliefs? You talk to your people about the organization's mission, about what it means to you personally. You explain how any given decision is related to that mission. You put yourself in your employees' shoes, just as you do with your customers; you ask what's important to them, and what the organization can do to meet those needs.

Then you make a genuine effort to deliver on those ideas—or explain why you can't. You set a high bar for performance, do everything you can to remove the barriers to your employees' success, and celebrate when they "do the ordinary things exceptionally well." You say thanks more often, and place blame less often.

Do these things day in and day out, and your employees will believe in you and your organization. Do these things and your employees will trust you, because you've earned their trust.

Management Reflections

Use this space to jot down answers to the following questions, and to outline any ideas, plans, or practical first steps you might take to move yourself or your organization forward.

1. *Do you think your organization's employees generally trust their leaders?*
2. *Can you think of specific decisions or actions that were taken in the past that might have led to employee dis-trust?*
3. *In those cases, could the organization's leaders made a different decision or acted differently? Do you think they (you) should take this different course?*

15. GOT GOOD JUDGMENT?

The dictionary defines "judgment" as "the ability to make a decision or form an opinion objectively, authoritatively, and wisely, especially in matters affecting action."

In every election year, we ask for many things in the person who eventually wins our vote. We ask for honesty, experience, and integrity—and we ask for good judgment. We want to know that our leaders will make the right decision and choose the right course of action when the pressure is on, the stakes are high, and there's either too much or too little information available. That's a lot to ask, and few people have met that high standard in every situation they've faced. As Will Rogers once said, "Good judgment comes from experience, and a lot of that comes from bad judgment."

But it's not just political leaders from whom we seek good judgment. We all hope to work in organizations in which the leaders consistently demonstrate an "ability to make a decision objectively, authoritatively, and wisely." And we all aspire to be that kind of leader ourselves.

During my career I've had the good fortune to work for and with a number of leaders who were highly respected for their ability to exercise good judgment in complex, high stakes situations. They were certainly different in style: some were introverted, others were charismatic; some relied heavily on "the data" while others seemed to act more intuitively. But when I think about it, they all had one thing in common: they all had the ability to imagine how each of the possible decisions on the table would actually affect a wide range of stakeholders they served. And they insisted that their advisors break out of the box of previous training and functional expertise to take a similarly broad view.

Peter Mercury, the GM of the Global Services Division at Digital/Compaq Computer/Hewlett Packard and one of the best servant-leaders I ever worked for, made this decision-making process very explicit. When faced with a complex problem—for example, whether to carry out a reduction in force, or to take money from the marketing budget to increase the spending on training—Peter would call his "kitchen cabinet" together. He'd ask for our input, ask questions, and encourage debate. And he'd ask us: "OK, if we put 100 people in a room—employees, stockholders, customers, partners—how am I going to explain to those folks why we made this particular decision? If I can't convince them all that this is the best decision we can make given what we know right now, then it's not the right decision."

So yes, good judgment definitely comes from experience and an ability to make sense of complex data. But I'm convinced that it also comes from a deep-seated commitment to caring for the people who will be affected by your decision. Like so many aspects of great leadership, it comes down to values.

What about you? Are you clear about the core values that guide your decision-making? When you're facing a tough decision, do you take the time to really think hard about its impact on the many constituencies you serve? I'd suggest that no matter how much pressure you're under to "just go ahead and make a decision," that would be time well spent.

Management Reflections

Use this space to jot down answers to the following questions, and to outline any ideas, plans, or practical first steps you might take to move yourself or your organization forward.

1. *Can you articulate your personal values?*
2. *If you asked for feedback about how you live these values, what do you think people would say?*

16. NEED MAJOR ORGANIZATIONAL CHANGE? DISSATISFACTION IS YOUR FRIEND!

Change is hard. Human beings seem to be hardwired to resist it. Before we can really commit ourselves to making a change in how we think or behave, we need to be seriously dissatisfied with things as they are.

Think about it. Have you ever made any significant change in your personal life—whether in a relationship, your weight or fitness level, your career, or just some habit you'd rather not have—without being deeply dissatisfied about that particular issue? People who have achieved the most difficult types of change—recovering from addiction, for example—typically talk about having to "hit bottom" before even being able to get started.

What's true for individuals is also true for organizations—which should come as no surprise, since organizations are made up of individuals, each "doing their own thing" in ways that don't always align very well with the organization's stated goals or preferred practices. So when the people in an organization generally feel that things are going well—when the sense is that the established ways of doing things are OK—achieving real change is next to impossible.

It comes down to, "Things could be better but we're still delivering results. Isn't that good enough? Why make a big change when things aren't broken?"

But leadership is about helping people and organizations get to a place they would not—could not—achieve by themselves. That's why leaders need to be appropriately paranoid about the future. They need to cultivate an ability to look past today's success, identify the challenges (and opportunities) that others might not see, and drive the changes necessary to deal with what's coming down the road.

Inevitably, that process involves identifying, leveraging—and when necessary, stimulating—dissatisfaction with the status quo. That doesn't mean that you as a leader run around like Chicken Little shouting that "the sky is falling." It certainly doesn't mean that you shouldn't recognize what your organization and its people are doing well. But it does mean that you need to point the way from good to great.

I like to take some of my clients through an exercise I call "Standing in the Future." I ask them to write a headline and an article for the *New York Times*, the *Wall Street Journal*, or their professional magazine that will appear five years from now. The article should discuss what their customers and shareholders think of their products, services, and employees. It should talk about how their employees feel about the company, and touch on the impact of the company on the communities where it operates, and on the larger world.

Then I ask them to identify three actions that will help them make dramatic progress towards that future in the next year. In all the times I've done it, this simple exercise has never failed to produce a very thought-provoking discussion.

If you're not satisfied with some aspects of your organization and its performance, you might try "standing in the future" and writing an article about what you see that others may not see. Then embrace the dissatisfaction this process may well create, and use it to get your organization mobilized!

Management Reflections

Use this space to jot down answers to the following questions, and to outline any ideas, plans, or practical first steps you might take to move yourself or your organization forward.

1. *Stand in the future, five years from now. How do you see yourself and your role in your organization?*
2. *What, if any, tension is there between that vision and where you are now?*
3. *What three steps could you take now to move closer to that vision?*

17. TURN YOUR MISSION STATEMENT INTO A CAUSE

In a 2015 *New York Times* opinion piece, Swarthmore Professor Barry Schwartz wrestled with the disheartening results from that year's Gallup engagement survey indicating that "almost 90 percent of workers were either 'not engaged' with or 'actively disengaged' from their jobs." In trying to figure out why this is so, Schwartz rejected the idea that "it's just human nature to dislike work" and that most of us work only for a paycheck. On the contrary, he argued:

Of course, we care about our wages, and we wouldn't work without them. But we care about more than money. We want work that is challenging and engaging, that enables us to exercise some discretion and control over what we do, and that provides us opportunities to learn and grow. We want to work with colleagues we respect and with supervisors who respect us. Most of all, we want work that is meaningful—that makes a difference to other people and thus ennobles us in at least some small way.

Take a look at that last sentence again: "Most of all, we want work that is meaningful—that makes a difference to other people and thus ennobles us in at least some small way."

When was the last time anyone in your organization took a look at your mission statement on your wall? Does its language pack an emotional wallop? Does it say—in a clear, compelling way—that the work of the organization is work that "makes a difference to other people and thus ennobles us in at least some small way"?

We're all looking for a cause—something we can give ourselves to with energy and passion. Many of us—and given the Gallup findings referenced above, I think we can say *most* of us—find our cause outside of work. We find it coaching Little League, volunteering at the local food pantry or hospice, or working for a political candidate. But typically, and sadly, we don't find it at work.

We've all heard the phrase, "It's just business; it's not personal." Think about that. I think this is just the opposite message leaders should be delivering. We should want our people to take the work they do very personally—whatever that work involves.

So how do you build this sense of purpose in your organization? How do you turn your mission statement into a cause? You start by getting your people involved. Give them a chance to sit with one another and talk about what the company does. How do the company's services or products make a difference to its customers? To the larger community? How does each function and role in the organization touch the customer? How does each *individual* touch and affect what the company does?

As one of my mentors used to say, "There are no back office jobs." What he meant is that every role in a business has an impact on the company's performance. Every role, even if it does not *directly* engage with the customer, has the potential to influence—for good or bad—how the customer perceives the company.

In other words, every job in the company is important. Every job has value and dignity. Get your people together and give them a chance to see that for themselves. Give them a chance to connect the dots between what they do and how the company contributes to its customers and the larger community. If you do that, you'll have taken a huge step toward bringing out the best in your people and your organization.

Virgin Atlantic Airways has what I consider a great mission statement: "to embrace the human spirit and let it fly." Why not get going on turning *your* mission statement into a cause. Get your people to fly!

Management Reflections

Use this space to jot down answers to the following questions, and to outline any ideas, plans, or practical first steps you might take to move yourself or your organization forward.

1. *Do your people feel connected to the organization's mission?*
2. *How often do talk about your mission during your staff meetings? Do those conversations create some emotion?*
3. *Do you ask customers to provide feedback or opinions about your mission statement?*

18. TREAT YOUR EMPLOYEES LIKE VOLUNTEERS: A STRANGE IDEA OR A KEY INSIGHT?

Have you ever worked for a not-for-profit organization that relies heavily on volunteers to accomplish its mission? Have you ever been a volunteer yourself? If so, you know just how deeply committed—and highly effective—volunteers can be. In fact, I think it's safe to say that most not-for-profits couldn't function without their volunteers. During my years at Cleveland Clinic, for example, I was continually amazed at the remarkable service provided to patients and their families by the hospital's more than 1000 volunteers.

What inspires these people to give up their time? They certainly feel a call to serve; they undoubtedly have a strong sense of purpose. But still, they could always give their time to some other organization. So you have to ask: how does an organization attract volunteers? How does it keep them committed? How does it keep them coming back? And how does a leader's behavior change when the people he or she leads can always just walk away?

In my experience, not-for-profit organizations go to great lengths to tell their story, in a way that gives volunteers a gut level connection with the people the organization serves and what it's trying to accomplish. They recognize their volunteers, tell stories about their contributions to the mission, and celebrate them as heroes.

Organizations that depend on volunteers don't manage by simply telling them what to do. Instead they manage with a 'light touch," explaining what needs to be done and how to do it, and providing ample support to help their volunteers succeed. Leaders in these organizations manage to tap into their volunteers' strengths, giving them a choice of how to participate and trying to make the work as much fun as possible. And again, most of all they find ways to thank their volunteers and let them know that without their efforts, the organization could not succeed or possibly even survive.

Now there's no doubt that to a great extent most of us go to work every day because that's how we pay the bills. Getting paid is a powerful motivator. But is compensation enough? Can money alone create engagement, that *"heightened emotional and intellectual connection that an employee has for their job, organization, manager, or co-workers that, in turn, influences them to apply additional discretionary effort to their work."*

There's a considerable body of research that indicates that money alone can't buy engagement. And on the flip side, not-for-profit organizations have demonstrated that engagement can be stimulated without money!

So think about these questions...

Management Reflections

Use this space to jot down answers to the following questions, and to outline any ideas, plans, or practical first steps you might take to move yourself or your organization forward.

1. *What if we did treat our employees like volunteers—as if they could just leave at any time?*
2. *How would we have to change as leaders and as an organization?*
3. *How would our people respond and what results could we achieve?*

19. GO SMALL OR GO HOME: DOING THE ORDINARY THINGS EXTRAORDINARILY WELL

How many times have you heard that the key to success is to "go big"? The conventional wisdom is that if you don't have the Big Idea, the Next Big Thing, The Breakthrough Idea, you'll never be a big winner. That's what it's all about right? You either think big or you go home.

I'd like to suggest something different. Thinking big is important, but unless you and your organization also think, value, and celebrate "small," you will never succeed!

Great teams focus on doing the ordinary things extraordinarily well. They obsess over the details. Why? Because that's the only way to turn a Big Idea from just an idea into an actual win on game day.

One of the most moving interviews I ever heard was with tennis star Pete Sampras after he beat three former US Open Champions to win his last US Open before retiring. He was at that time, and still may be, arguably the best tennis player in history. He was asked during the interview what he thought was the key to his success. Pete, never a person to use a lot of words, simply said "I just worked really hard at my game and was able to do the ordinary things extraordinarily well I guess!"

Again, great athletes, great leaders in any field, and great organizations do the ordinary things extraordinary well. Don't get me wrong. "Go big or go home" has its place when you're "standing in the future" to create a compelling vision for yourself or your organization. You have to dream big, and paint a vivid picture of what success entails, or you won't get to experience that success. But unless you focus on the details, the ordinary things that end up leading to extraordinary results, you're going home.

Successful organizations have learned to harness the power of big ideas by knowing they come to reality by thinking small.

Have you ever sat in a meeting and have someone present a strategy by saying, "Here's my idea for a new strategy. It's a loser but I'm presenting it anyway"? Of course you haven't, because every strategy sounds like a winning strategy. But often, the difference between a winning and losing strategy is the ability to execute. In order to execute well, you have to get small. I'd be willing to bet that your last great customer experience didn't come because someone did something heroic for you. It much more likely came as a result of an ordinary interaction in which the other person took great care to make every little detail go perfectly.

I've been working with organizations for over thirty years, helping them build engaged enterprises. We often start at the enterprise level, rolling out a new big idea or program, and there's no doubt that what happens and what gets communicated at that level is critically important. But in the end real progress only comes when we get small, because building engagement is a local phenomenon.

It happens when every manager, in every unit in every division, builds plans with their people and executes on those plans. It happens when leaders and employees at every level take responsibility for making their organization a great place to work. It happens when leaders at every level come to understand the power of a simple thank you when they see someone doing an ordinary thing extraordinarily well. It happens when leaders learn that taking the time to know their people on a personal level is time well spent. It happens when leaders recognize that there are no back offices in any organization, when they believe and make everyone else believe that everybody's work is critical to the success of the organization.

Management Reflections

Use this space to jot down answers to the following questions, and to outline any ideas, plans, or practical first steps you might take to move yourself or your organization forward.

1. *When and how have you gotten "small" with your people?*
2. *How you recognize and celebrate your people's small, everyday successes?*

20. IT'S NOT ABOUT YOUR PERSONAL BRAND

Many self-improvement gurus—folks like Tom Peters—would suggest that one step we absolutely must take if we want to succeed in life is to create a powerful "personal brand." Writing in *Fast Company* back in 1997, Peters said:

Regardless of age, regardless of position, regardless of the business we happen to be in, all of us need to understand the importance of branding. We are CEOs of our own companies: Me Inc. To be in business today, our most important job is to be head marketer for the brand called You.

Google "personal brand" today and you'll come up with over 68 million hits; check out Amazon and you'll find over 300,000 books promising to help you craft or improve your personal brand.

I can't say that I'm crazy about the term *personal brand* itself, because contrary to what Mr. Peters and others say, I find it hard to think about people the same way I think of laundry detergent or running shoes or any other product. I also have a problem with much of what's written about "personal branding" because so much of it is about crafting an image of yourself and getting maximum visibility for that image in the market place. It's like selling Tide detergent or Nike shoes.

Of course what others think about you is important. Your personal reputation (my preferred term) walks in the room ahead of you, and often shapes whether or not people in that room are willing to listen to you, trust you, or follow you. But that's not about image. No—you build a reputation that inspires trust not by worrying about your image, but by treating others with the respect and dignity they deserve, by helping them succeed, by delivering on the promises you make. You build a reputation that inspires trust by *not* focusing first on yourself.

So let me suggest that instead of working on your personal brand, you work on yourself as a person. We could all benefit from asking ourselves questions like these:

- What are my personal core values?
- What values motivate me to do the work I'm doing?
- Do I consistently live my values, in the actions I take and the decisions I make?
- Do I listen to others more than I talk about myself?
- Do I consistently look for ways to help others succeed?

I think success in life—which certainly includes success in your career—is to consistently live your values and consistently help others succeed. Do that and people will perceive you as someone who can be counted on to make the right decisions in difficult situations. Do that and they'll view you as a values-driven person—someone driven by a higher sense of purpose rather than a desire to polish your "brand." Do that and you'll be respected because you respect others, because you take the time listen to them, instead of just looking for ways to advance your own opinions. Do that and you'll build a personal reputation that inspires others to believe in you, trust you, and follow you.

Do that and you won't have to worry about your personal brand.

Management Reflections

Use this space to jot down answers to the following questions, and to outline any ideas, plans, or practical first steps you might take to move yourself or your organization forward.

1. *How do you think the people in your organization perceive you? What specific situations can you recall that can help you get an objective answer to this critical question?*
2. *The chances are that people perceive you as having both positive and negative traits. What might you do to begin addressing those that are seen as negative?*

ABOUT JOSEPH M. PATRNCHAK

PRINCIPAL, GREEN SUMMIT PARTNERS, LLC

Joe Patrnchak is head of Green Summit Partners, a consulting practice dedicated to helping organizations bring out the best in their people.

Prior to establishing Green Summit, Joe served as Chief Human Resources Officer at Cleveland Clinic. Tasked with making the Clinic a great place to work and grow, building a highly engaged workforce, and modernizing the HR function, he:

■ Led development of a "we are all caregivers" culture—with innovative serving leadership, employee wellness, and recognition programs—that drove engagement to world class levels (as measured by Gallup), and contributed to a dramatically improved patient experience (as measured by Federal "HCHAPS" results).

■ Implemented a new "people strategy" that transformed the Clinic into an employer of choice—recognized by numerous local, regional, and national awards.

■ Directed deployment of HR best practices and a 21st century delivery platform that greatly improved HR services.

Before joining Cleveland Clinic in 2007, Joe served as Chief HR Officer and Senior Vice President at Blue Cross Blue Shield of Massachusetts. At BCBSMA, he played a key role in reenergizing this mature organization through new strategic planning, performance management, and leadership development processes, and through innovative work-life, career development, and employee health programs that improved engagement to benchmark levels.

Previously, Joe served as VP of Human Resources for HP/Compaq/Digital, including leading HR for the $4.5B Global Customer Services Division, cited by IDC, Gartner, and Forrester as the technology industry's #1 or #2 service business.

Joe holds an MS in Human Resources Management and Organizational Development from American University; he is also a graduate of the Advanced Executive Program at Northwestern University's Kellogg School, and the International Management Program at INSEAD, Fontainebleau France. He holds a BA in Sociology from Northwestern, where he (along with his twin brother Carl) was defensive co-captain of the football team and a member of the All Big Ten Academic Team.

A co-Founder of the Healthcare Human Resources Forum, and a frequent conference speaker, he is the author of *The Engaged Enterprise: A Field Guide for the Servant-Leader*, as well as journal articles on organizational change, rewards & recognition, employee engagement, and servant leadership.

Joe is active in a number of community service organizations and religious ministries, including serving as a Board Member of the Robert Greenleaf Center for Servant Leadership; Cleveland Inner City Tennis Clinics; Tenacity, Inc.; and the Oblates of the Virgin Mary.

Joe divides his time between his Boston home and Vermont log cabin. He is an avid skier, tennis player, and fly fisherman.

Find out more about Joe and Green Summit Partners at WWW.GSUMMIT.CO.

Also look for *The Engaged Enterprise: A Field Guide for the Servant-Leader* by Joseph M. Patrnchak

Made in the USA
Columbia, SC
13 April 2021